# DEDICATION

A 37-Day Guide from Heartbreak to Healing is dedicated to all the men and women who have suffered painful heartbreaks and have chosen to seek healing and understanding. This book is for all those who have decided not to give up on love, but merely to love smarter.

# INTRODUCTION

Break-up Breakthrough A 37-Day Guide from Heartbreak to Healing was created to give you the tools to use your relationship break-up as the motivation to transform your life and position yourself to attract the love that you need. Break-up Breakthrough will guide you over 37 days to look at you, your relationship patterns, how those patterns came to be, as well as how your patterns have influenced your relationship choices. The daily exercises and assignments will help you to honestly look at yourself and how your past may have contributed to the relationship you chose. The intention of this book is to help you find the loving relationship you deserve.

If you follow the steps outlined in Break-up Breakthrough you will acquire the tools necessary to help repair your broken pieces and attract a person who will appreciate your uniqueness and nurture your spirit.

During the next 37 days, you will come face to face with yourself in a way that will expose your patterns, heartaches, frustrations, past trauma, what you feel about yourself and the relationship blunders that you have made in the past. You will discover your patterns of attraction, motivations, family issues, your wants vs. your needs, your relationship styles, your methods of self-abuse, your blind spots, how you may have given yourself away too cheaply. It can also reveal, who you are in relationships and what you need to do to get back on the right track. The questions and exercises will give you the tools to help yourself get very clear on where you went wrong in your previous relationships and what you can do to be better and attract a better and more appropriate partner, someone who is good to you and good for you. If you allow yourself to go deep inside yourself and acknowledge, feel and forgive, then you will realize that this process is where your healing and breakthrough will be found.

This Break-up Breakthrough Workbook was designed to be used in conjunction with the Break-up Breakthrough book. The workbook will accelerate your healing process and provide deeper insights into all the areas that need to be examined in order to find the Breakthrough you desire. You will find exercises for 37 days, each corresponding to the same subject matter as that day in the Break-up Breakthrough book. The process works best if you read the specific day of the book then work the exercises in the workbook for that day. Space has been left for you to write about your thoughts and any insights that you may glean from the process, as well as any emotions that may arise as a result of the exercises. Please put your thoughts, emotions, past hurts and revelations on paper. Make every attempt to address what you feel, PLEASE do not try to hide your emotions in the back of your mind, they can hurt you there. If you expose them, you can properly address them, analyze them and loosen their grip on your life, self-esteem and decision making. As long as the monster is in the closet you will be afraid, but when it is exposed you will realize that it is has no power over you.

Working the exercises designated for each day will of course expose some emotions that will probably be painful, but it will also provide some valuable insights that will help you grow and flourish. In the pages of this workbook you will come face-to-face with yourself in a way that will expose your patterns, heartaches, frustrations, past trauma, what you feel about yourself and the relationship blunders that you have made in the past. You will discover your patterns of attraction, motivations, family issues, your wants vs. your needs, your relationship styles, your methods of self abuse, your blind spots, etc. The questions and exercises outlined in this workbook will give you the tools to better understand where you went wrong in your previous relationships and what you can do to improve and attract a better and more appropriate partner. Take your time each day and give some thought to the questions, dig deep beneath the surface and feel whatever emotions come up. I will caution you again, because it is so important! Please do not try to push your emotions back into your subconscious mind. When your emotions are out in the open, you can examine them and learn the lessons attached to each one of these emotions. If you allow yourself to go deep inside yourself and acknowledge, feel and forgive, then you will realize that this process is where your healing and breakthrough will be found.

Break-up Breakthrough provides the questions that you need to answer to truly understand your relationship patterns and personal history. It requires you to engage in honest and truthful self-assessment which enables you to gather the insights that you need. Each day you will peel off another layer from the onion that has been the source of your heartbreak and despair, and as you know any time you peel an onion there will be some tears. But on the other side there will be insights, unconscious knowledge that becomes conscious, a clear idea of what you need as opposed to what you want and a plan and strategy that will help you find and locate the love that you desire and deserve.

If you approach each day with honesty and embrace the vulnerability that might arise, in the next 37 days you will be on your way to discovering the relationship that fulfills your dreams and the bliss that is your birthright.

The lessons you will learn from the Break-up Breakthrough Book and the Break-up Breakthrough Workbook will provide you with much needed information to help repair your broken places, see how your past influences your future, change your mind and your agenda and help you develop the skills to attract a person who will appreciate your uniqueness and nurture your spirit.

Take the trip; it will be arduous at the beginning and joyous at the end. If you do the work you will get the results you desire and revamp your life as a result. Sometimes it will feel like a roller-coaster ride, but as usual you enjoy and appreciate the ride much more after it is finished. Your healing and your Breakthrough awaits; only you have the option to choose it. I pray you will accept this challenge.

Blessings to you, I'm sending Love and Light your way.

# DAY 1
*It's Your Party, Cry if You Want To*

In the space below, express your emotions surrounding your most recent break-up.

Be honest about your feelings. What hurts the most?

What realizations must you face?

Write until you feel empty and allow yourself time and space to grieve.

# DAY 2
*ACT OUT-- GET EVEN*

List at least three lessons that you have learned about yourself as a result of this relationship.

1.

2.

3.

What did you learn about how you act and react in relationships?

What is the worst thing you've done in an attempt to get even in a relationship?

What consequences did you endure as a result of your actions?

How did it make you feel?

Other than yourself, who did you hurt?

Do you feel as if you still harbor negative energy as a result of these actions? If so please list them.

What are some things that you can do to clear the negative energy of this relationship?

Write at least three goals that you want to work on to have a better relationship.

1.

2.

3.

# DAY 3
*Resign Yourself*
*Don't Play 20 Questions*

Please answer the following questions honestly.

What do you tell yourself about this relationship?




What is the truth about it?




What do you not want to admit to yourself?




Is there an "If only" that you have struggled with in this relationship?

Do you think that things would have been different if your "If only" were true?

What type of things have you done in an attempt to extend a relationship?

What were the consequences of those actions?

How can you use the lesson learned from this relationship to improve yourself?

# DAY 4

*Confess --Analyze*
THE 411

Think about your most recent relationship and past relationships and list any clues you may have missed or decided to ignore?

What are the things that are obvious now, that you previously did not to see during the relationship?

Who did you think your partner was?

Who was he/she in reality?

Analyze the clues that you missed and the things that you decided not to see in your last three relationships.

# DAY 5
*Will the Real You Please Step Forward?*

Did you reveal your "REAL" self in your most recent relationship? If not, how did you present yourself?

Did you try to be the person that you thought your partner wanted?

If so, in what ways were you inauthentic?

If so, in what ways were you inauthentic? Were your wants, needs and desires replaced with your partner's?

If so, how does this practice usually manifest itself in your relationships?

Do you believe that you will not be loved if you are completely yourself?

If so, why do you believe that?

What part of yourself do you tend to give up in relationships?

Do you give up your friends?

Have you ever faked being compatible with someone that you knew you were not compatible with?

If so, why?

Your assignment for today is to list the ways in which you tend to compromise yourself in relationships.

# DAY 6

*The Teacher and the Lesson Plan*

Your assignment for today is to analyze what your romantic relationships have in common and how they compare to patterns that you have seen in your family.

What did you like about this relationship?

What were the major distasteful characteristics of this relationship?

How did he/she treat you?

How did being with him/her make you feel about yourself?

Have you ever had these feelings before?

What was it about him/her that attracted you?

Have you ever felt like this in any other relationship in your life?

What are five similarities that you can point out in your most recent relationships?

# DAY 7
*You AGAIN*

Are there any similarities between what you experienced as a child and what you experienced in your romantic relationships?

How do you recreate your childhood scenario in relationships?

How would you describe the man/woman you always date?

Do you date the same man/woman with a different name?

# DAY 8
*Knowing You*

Your assignment for today is to make a list of the people that you have dated. Next to each name, make a list of all the things that attracted you to this person.

What were the motivating factors in the relationship and how did your partner make you feel?

As a result of the relationship, were you closer or further away from your goals? Be careful to note the emergence of any patterns.

Are there any common emotions from your relationships that were also present in your family history?

# DAY 9
*The Order Form*

List five improvements you can make on how you love and nurture yourself?

1.
2.
3.
4.
5.

How do you nourish your mind and spirit?

How do you want your lover to treat you?

How can you teach your lover to treat you the way that you want to be treated?

What do you want to put on the order form for your next relationship?

# DAY 10

*Changing Expectations*
*The What? When? Why?*

Today you are going to work on recognizing the reason, season and lesson from your last relationships. Your assignment is to analyze your last five relationships.

What did each relationship teach you?

What was the reason for getting involved in each of these relationships?

What did all five relationships have in common?

Who were you in these relationships?

How were the relationships different? How were they the same?




How were you different? How were you the same?




Who were you in the face of the break-up?

# DAY 11
*Knowing the Unknown*
I SEE YOU

What are some things that you do that can be considered as destructive?

What are the things you do to yourself that a person in love with himself or herself wouldn't do?

How did you feel about yourself as a child, a teenager and young adult?

What led you to believe these things?

Make a list of the things that you want to work on to nourish your mind, body and Spirit.

Take one item on that list and decide to work on it for 30 days. What strategy will you use?

# DAY 12

*The Honesty Muscle*
*The GOOD, BAD and the UGLY*

What is the truth about your life and relationships?

What is your good, bad and ugly?

What circumstances from your childhood and teenage years are you recreating in your adult relationships?

Where are you broken?

List the truths that you need to admit to yourself?

# DAY 13
*Leaving the Past*

Is there something in your past that you need to forgive yourself or others for?

How has not forgiving these things affected you?

Is it possible that not forgiving yourself, your past lover, parent or another person can be holding you back from the love you want and need?

Observation exercise:
Your assignment is to go to a public place (festival, mall, nightclub, concert, restaurant, park etc.) and merely watch people. Find the perfect spot and be the silent observer for an hour or two. Observe how people act. What do you think they think about themselves based on their actions? What do you think other people watching would think of them? Did anyone in the crowd remind you about how you act?

What did you learn from the observing the people that you watched?

Can you apply any of these lessons to your life?

Develop a plan to make sure your behavior tells the truth about who you are.

# DAY 14
*Using the Past for Inspiration*
*Kissing Frogs*

Your assignment for today is to examine your most recent relationships. Answer the following questions.

When did you know this was not the right relationship for you?

How long did you wait until you did something about it?

What did you endure as a result of waiting?

What were the consequences?

Make a list of your major relationship mistakes.

# DAY 15
*Recognizing GOOD LOVE*
*20/20*

Your assignment for today is to chose three people or couples to interview about their relationships using the questions outlined in Break-up Breakthrough. Schedule your interviews to last no more than one hour and when they are complete write a summary on each couple or individual based on the insights that you gathered.

# DAY 16
*A New Attitude*

What is your worldview?

What does a normal relationship look like according to your worldview?

What is the role of a woman in a relationship?

What is the role of a man in a relationship?

How have your partner's views differed from yours?

Whose views were right and whose views were wrong?

# DAY 17
*The Million-Dollar Question*
*Jeopardy*

Make a list of the things that you would like to know about a potential partner from the onset.

Develop a list of questions that you can ask to gather the information you desire.

Commit your most important questions to memory.

# DAY 18

*Knowing Better and Doing Better*
ACTION

Write a couple of paragraphs to describe who you think you are. Then ask two or three people that know you well if it is an accurate description. Ask them what they would add or subtract from your synopsis.

Create a space where your friends can be brutally honest. You will learn how people really see and experience you. This information will be critical in developing your plans to be a better version of you.

# DAY 19
*Sphere of Influence*
*Blind Spots*

Make a list of the people who have been the most supportive and influential in your life.

Determine who has given you the best advice over time without trying to control you. Who has loved you through your mistakes?

From this list, determine who your relationship consultants or Sphere of Influence will be.

Then decide the ground rules regarding their input.

Write a short statement outlining the role you will ask your Sphere of Influence to play in your Breakthrough.

## DAY 20
*Evaluating Your Needs*
*Spinach or Ice Cream*

What are your short-term and long-term relationship goals?

What is your Spinach (your needs)?

What is your Ice Cream (wants)?

Are there places where your wants and needs intercept?

Which is more important to you?

# DAY 21

*The Makeover*
*Until Today*

What does your dream relationship look like?

How does it make you feel?

What kind of person is he/she?

Who are you in this relationship?

How do you stay completely authentic in this relationship?

How do you love, support and nourish your partner?

How are you loved, supported and nourished?

What do you have to learn to make a relationship like this successful?

What are your Deal Breakers?

What are your expectations?

Explain why you deserve a relationship like the one you want.

# DAY 22
*Profiling*

Write a profile of your dream mate

# DAY 23
*Getting Realistic*

Revise the profile of your dream mate. Carefully examine what you wrote yesterday and get completely clear and realistic. Was there anything that you wrote that is unrealistic? Determine what is a "must-have" and what is not and modify your profile

What did you change and why?

## DAY 24
*Knowing Your Worth*
*Deserving or NO*

Identify the relationships in your life that deplete your energy and leave you feeling used or abused.

Identify the relationships in your life that energize, support and nourish you.

Are there any relationships that need to be renegotiated or ended?

Was there ever a time when you went after the 10% group? What happened? What lessons did you learn?

Is there anyone is the 90% group that you may have overlooked or taken for granted?

## DAY 25
*A New Attitude*
*Setting Your Agenda*

What is your love agenda?

What are you hoping to accomplish with your new relationship?

Have there been times in a relationship when you compromised your safety, freedom, life or health?

What were the results?

How would you handle a similar situation today?

## DAY 26
*What I Really, Really Want.*

List the times that you ignored what was right in front of you?

What were the consequences that you have endured as a result?

What is your plan to ensure that this does not happen again?

# DAY 27

*Communicating*
*Standing In Your Truth*

On what occasions have you not used your words to express your wants, needs, hurts or disappointments?

List several instances when you thought your partner should have understood why you were upset or hurt and he/she didn't.

How did you express your hurt to him/her? Did you pout? Blow-up? Give the silent treatment? Withhold sex?

Did your methods of expressing your hurt produce the response you expected?

How could you have used your words and effective communication techniques to get what you wanted?

How do you plan to keep open, effective communication going in your new relationships?

What are the things that you think you and your partner must agree on for a healthy, mutually satisfying relationship?

# DAY 28

*The Choice*
*To Have or to Let Go*

Now that you are single, where do you go from here?

Do you go back to your old relationship patterns or do you hold out for the loving, nurturing relationship that you dream about?

How will you deal with your loneliness while waiting on the right partner?

Will you accept seat-fillers?

**BREAK-UP BREAKTHROUGH**
A 37-DAY GUIDE FROM HEARTBREAK TO HEALING
WORKBOOK

## DAY 29
*Counting the Cost*

Examine your last three relationships and calculate the cost of each relationship in:

- Time
- Money
- Education
- Child Support
- Career Advancement
- Social Standing
- Respect from your children
- Family Relations and Friendships
- Personal Peace

# DAY 30
*Relationship Styles*

What has been the relationship style of the majority of your relationships?

Did the relationship's dynamics change over time?

What happened when there was need to renegotiate the roles in the relationship?

What type of relationship style do you think will be most fulfilling for you in the long run?

## DAY 31

*Knowing how to Break It*
*Hitting the Reset Button*

How have you ended relationships in the past?

How have your exes ended relationships with you?

What is an effective way of ending a relationship?




Did your methods of ending a relationship destroy the relationship completely, or were you able to agree and move on amicably?




What steps can you take to ensure that you end a relationship with dignity?

## DAY 32

*MINE, Mine and Mine*
*Protecting Your Resources*

Evaluate your last five relationships using the concept of sharing versus taking. Which partners do you feel were sharers and which ones were takers?

How long did it take you to recognize the difference between a sharer and a taker?

Can you name specific incidents that made it clear that your partner was a sharer or a taker?

What can you do to discover which category potential partner should fall into at the beginning of a relationship?

# DAY 33
*Normal or Not*

What's your idea of a normal relationship?

How much of what you wrote do you believe is actually realistic?

Are any of your views outdated?

How will you negotiate a new normal when life presents relationship challenges?

# DAY 34
*Which Flower*

When you meet a new potential partner, how do you react? Do you start planning the wedding in your head or do you relax and let the relationship mature naturally?

What steps can you take to make sure you see who this person is before getting too attached?

Have there been times when you moved too fast?

What were the results of moving too fast?

What can you do to let the relationship naturally mature?

# DAY 35
*Quantity vs. Quality*

Have you most often had quality or quantity in your past relationships?

What would you like in your next relationship?

How will you know the difference?

**BREAK-UP BREAKTHROUGH**
A 37-DAY GUIDE FROM HEARTBREAK TO HEALING
WORKBOOK

## DAY 36

*Take a Deep Breath*
*Learning in Action*

Your assignment for today is to make a list of activities, places, classes, community events or places to volunteer that you can participate in that will broaden your horizons and place you in a position to meet new and interesting people.

What are you going to do to put your best foot forward?

How are you going to show your authentic personality?

What advice would you give to someone experiencing heartbreak?

What lessons would like to share with others?

# DAY 37
*Lessons Learned*

What are the most important lessons that you learned about relationships?

What advice would you give to someone experiencing heartbreak?

What lessons would like to share with others?

# LAST THINGS

Today, I hope that you will take the time to stop and think about the process, the exercises, and the lessons you have learned. Think carefully, what did you learn about you, about relationships, about your wants and needs? Take the time to write these lessons down so that you can go back to them easily and remind yourself when your days become difficult and you're lonely and thinking that you may never find the love of your life.

Modify your Plan and update your process as regularly as you need to. Be ready when the right relationship comes your way.

Share your insights on my website at www.JaniceMoss.com

Share an insight that might make another person's journey easier. Share your failures and your successes. The cost you paid in relationships and the insights you've had. Please share:

- What questions should you ask yourself before getting into another relationship?
- What do you know now that you wish you had known then?
- How have you picked up the pieces?
- What was the hardest part for you?
- Did it get easier?
- What advice would you give?
- Will you share these insights and tell your secrets so we all can go on improving?

Made in the USA
Middletown, DE
19 September 2016